DISENCHANTED

MUSIC FROM THE MOTION PICTURE SOUNDTRACK

MUSIC BY
ALAN MENKEN

LYRICS BY
STEPHEN SCHWARTZ

ISBN 978-1-70518-689-3

Motion Picture Artwork, TM & Copyright © 2022 Disney

HAL•LEONARD®

Visit Hal Leonard Online at
www.halleonard.com

World headquarters, contact:
Hal Leonard
7777 West Bluemound Road
Milwaukee, WI 53213
Email: info@halleonard.com

In Europe, contact:
Hal Leonard Europe Limited
1 Red Place
London, W1K 6PL
Email: info@halleonardeurope.com

In Australia, contact:
Hal Leonard Australia Pty. Ltd.
4 Lentara Court
Cheltenham, Victoria, 3192 Australia
Email: info@halleonard.com.au

CONTENTS

EVEN MORE ENCHANTED

Music by ALAN MENKEN
Lyrics by STEPHEN SCHWARTZ

Quickly

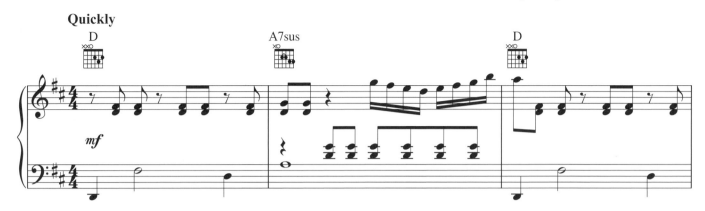

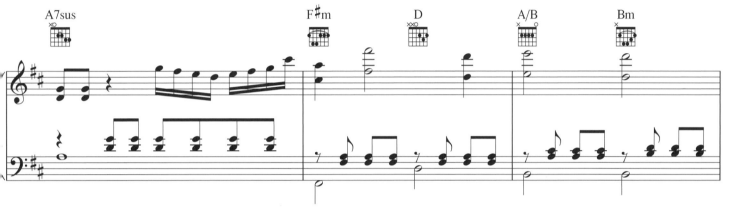

Here we are, our fam-'ly start-ing o - ver where life will be nic - er and new - er now.

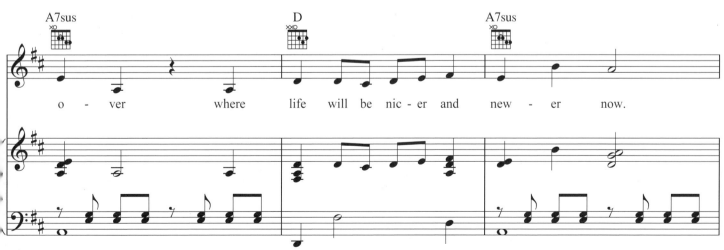

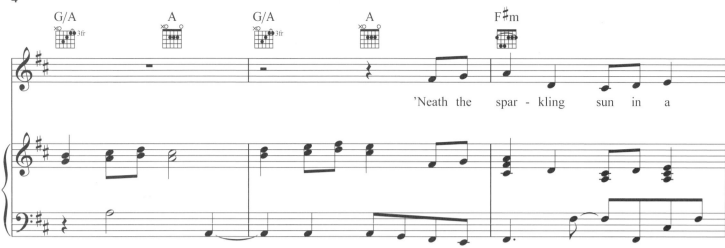

'Neath the spar-kling sun in a

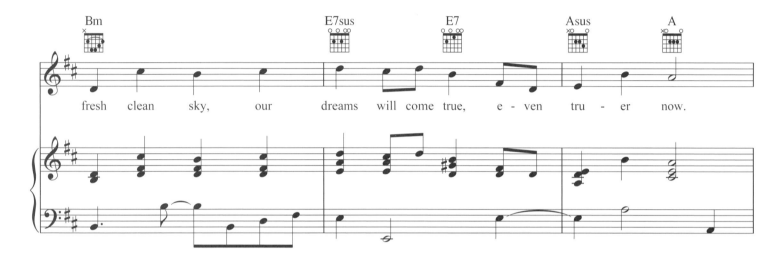

fresh clean sky, our dreams will come true, e-ven tru-er now.

In a yard that's full of four-leaf

clo-ver, we'll bloom where we've been trans-plant-ed. And

life will be brim-ming with e - ven more joy in store

than be - fore. _____ And e - ven more en -

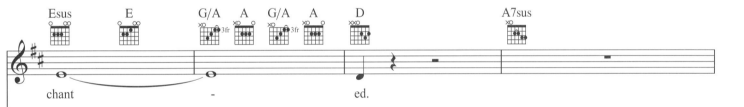

chant - ed.

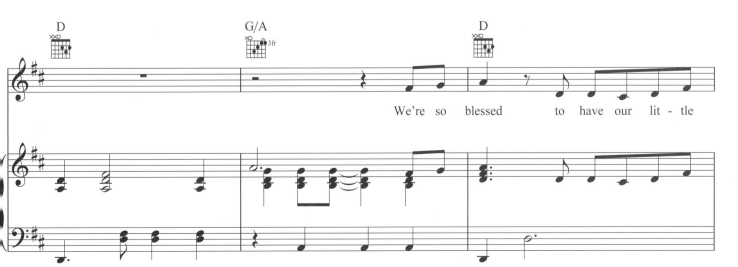

We're so blessed to have our lit - tle

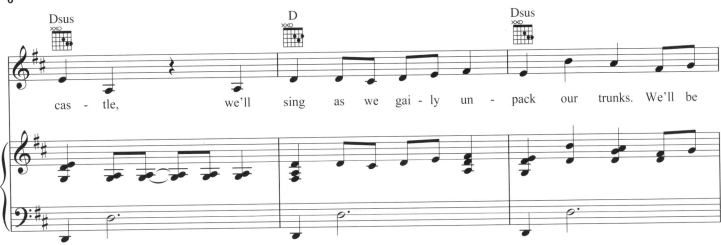

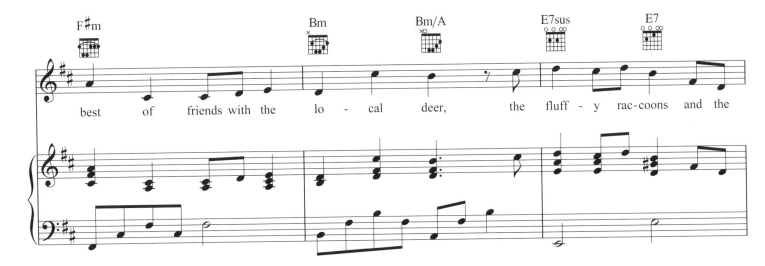

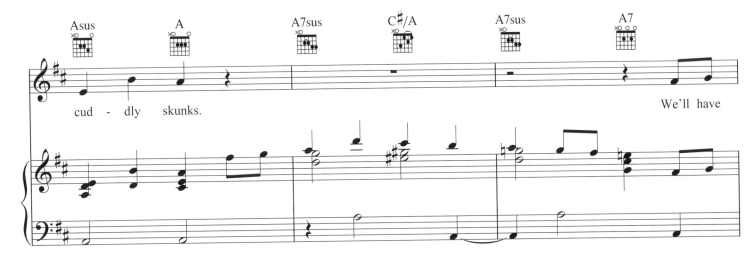

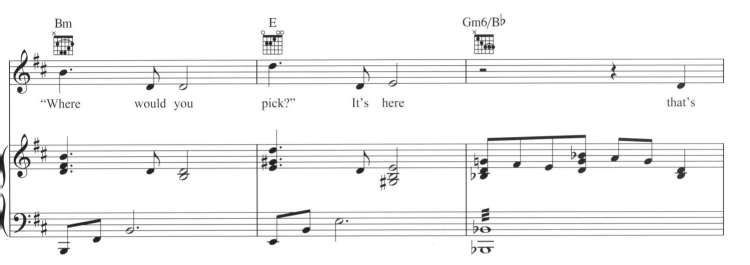

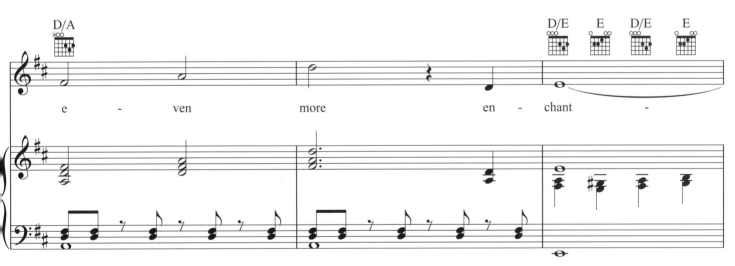

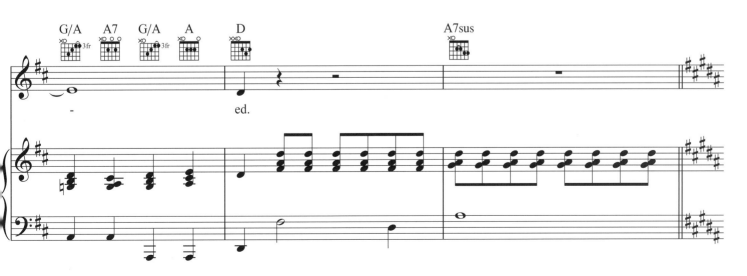

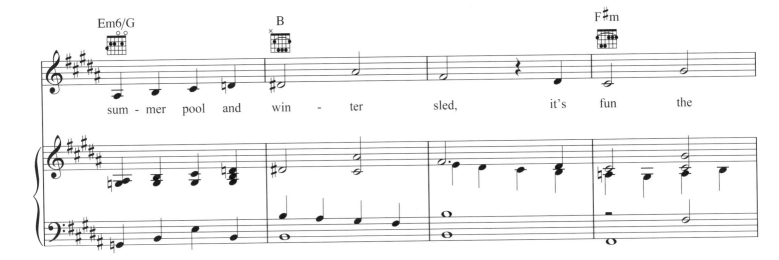

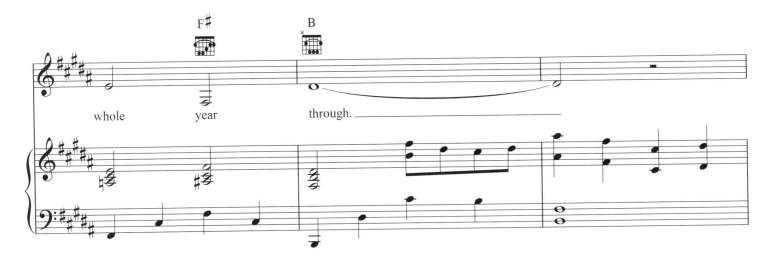

With an a - bove - ground sum - mer pool and win - ter sled, it's fun the whole year through. ___ Neigh - bors who are so friend - ly that they're in - t'rest -

C#7sus C#7

ed in ev - 'ry - thing we

A7 A7sus D

do! _____ Far a - way from all the noise and

A7sus D D9

has - sle, our wish - es will all be grant - ed. And

G D/F# Bm

e - ven the nas - ti - est birds will tweet ex - tra sweet.

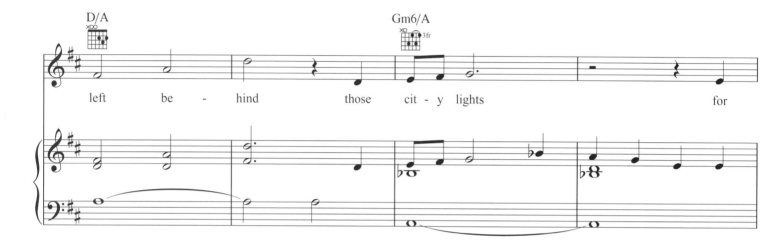

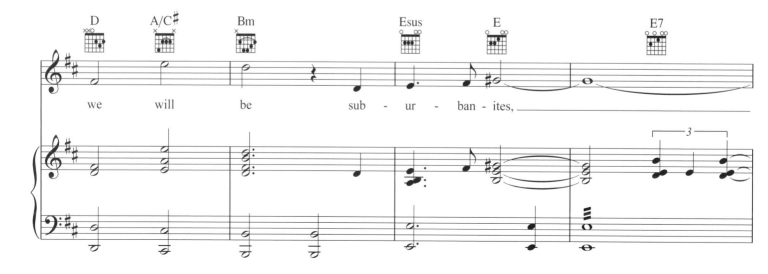

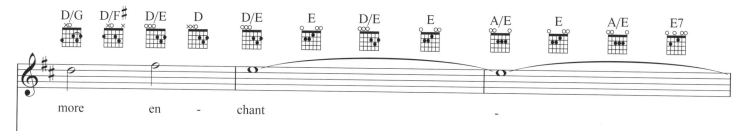

THE MAGIC OF ANDALASIA

Music by ALAN MENKEN
Lyrics by STEPHEN SCHWARTZ

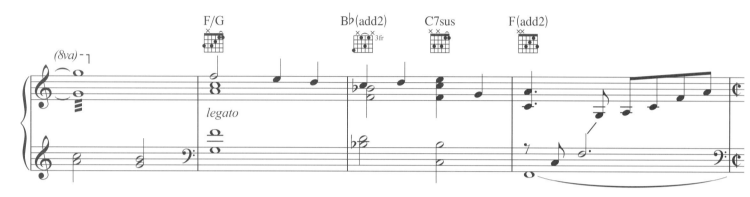

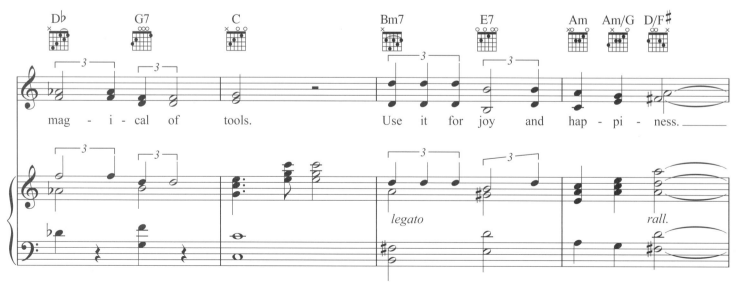

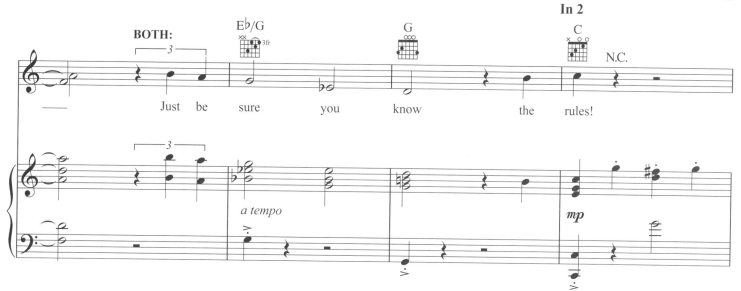

Just be sure you know the rules!

Here's the mag - ic

of An - da - la - sia, con - tained in this won - 'drous wish - ing

wand. We bring some mag - ic

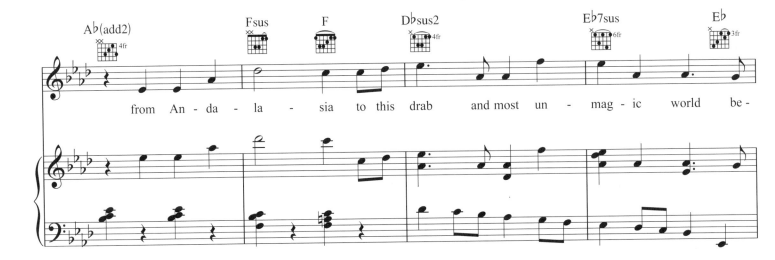

from An - da - la - sia to this drab and most un - mag - ic world be -

yond! **NANCY:** This wish - ing wand she will

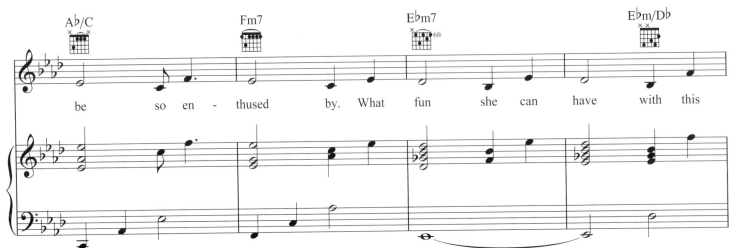

be so en - thused by. What fun she can have with this

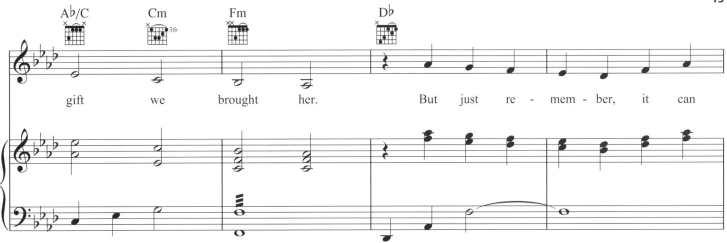

gift we brought her. But just re- mem- ber, it can

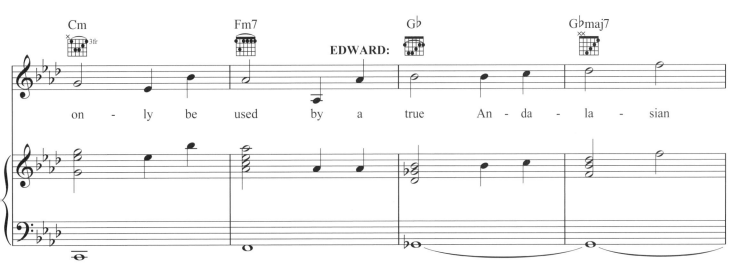

EDWARD:

on- ly be used by a true An- da- la- sian

NANCY:

son or daugh - ter. _____

mp

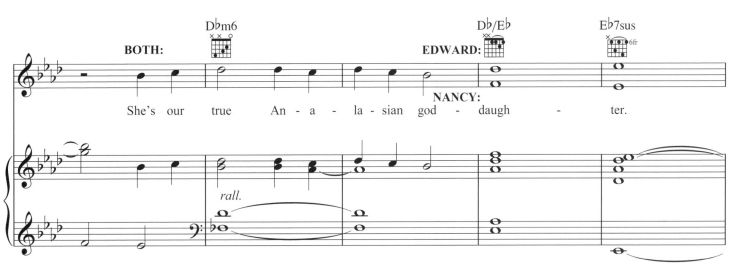

BOTH:

EDWARD:

NANCY:

She's our true An - a - la- sian god- daugh - ter.

rall.

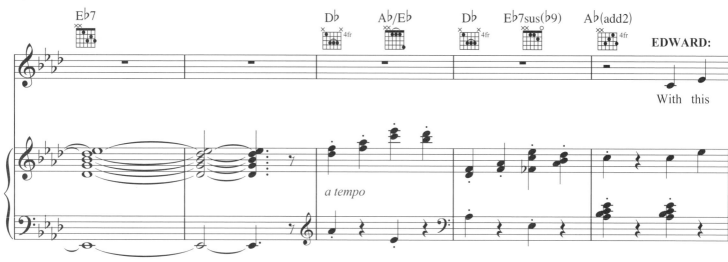

she'll use the mag - ic of An - da - la - sia.

EDWARD: And if she has ques - tions, just con - sult this scroll!

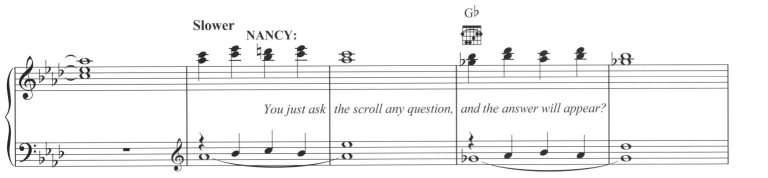

Slower **NANCY:** *You just ask the scroll any question, and the answer will appear?*

EDWARD: *Or I suppose in this land you just read it?* *How do you live in this place?*

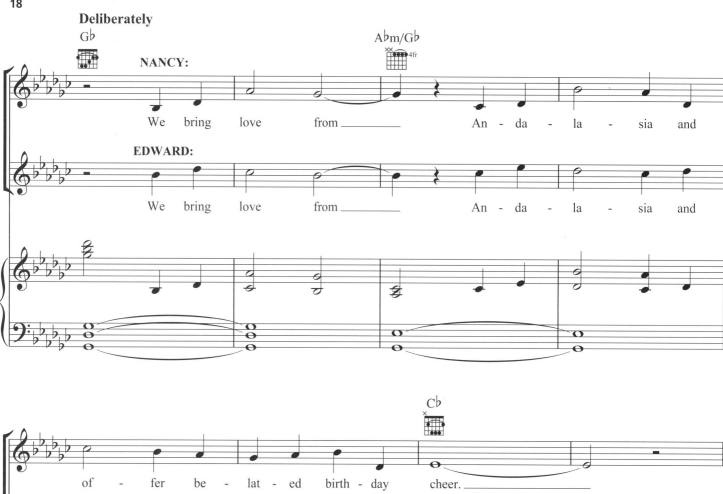

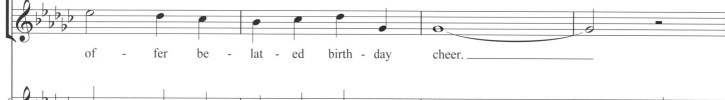

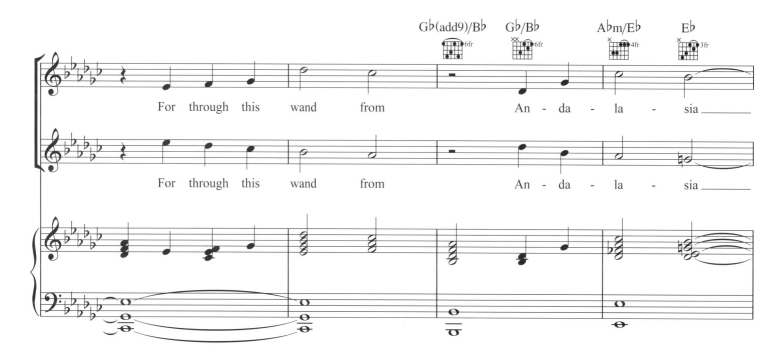

An - da - la - sia

An - da - la - sia

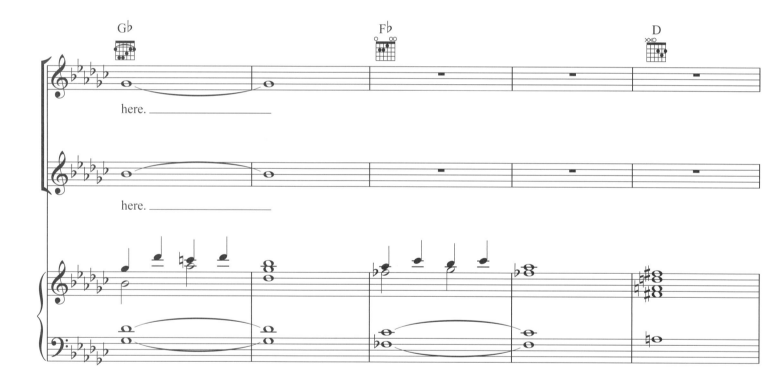

here. _____

here. _____

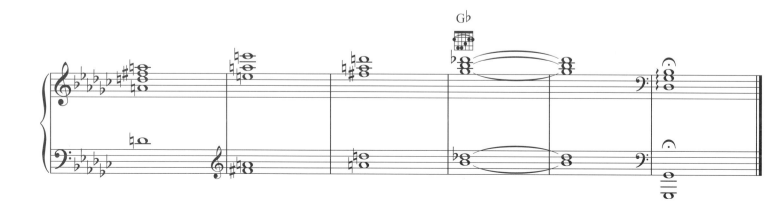

FAIRYTALE LIFE
(The Wish)

Music by ALAN MENKEN
Lyrics by STEPHEN SCHWARTZ

Flowing Ballad

Once up-on a time, back there in An-da-la-sia, rules were clear and col-ors did-n't fade. And once you found your hap-p'ly ev-er af-ter, your hap-p'ly ev-er af-ter al-ways stayed. And then I jour-neyed here, where

true love's kiss was wait-ing; met my prince, be-came his prin-cess wife. But was

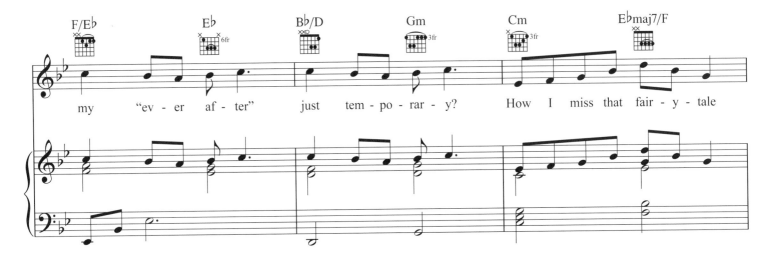

my "ev-er af-ter" just tem-po-rar-y? How I miss that fair-y-tale

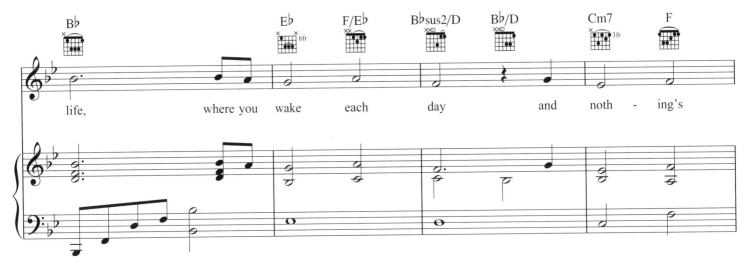

life, where you wake each day and noth-ing's

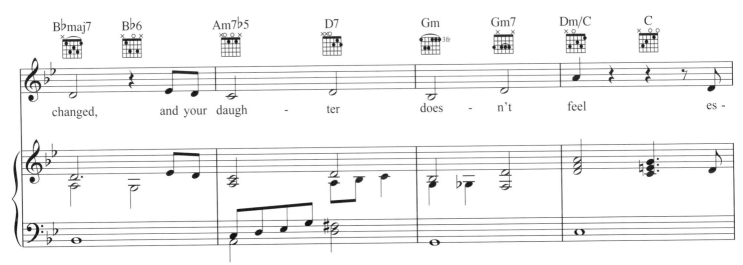

changed, and your daugh-ter does-n't feel es-

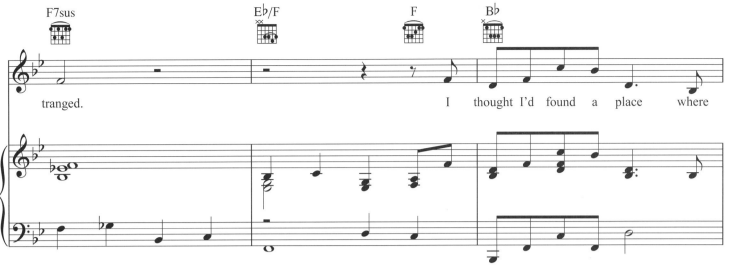

tranged. I thought I'd found a place where

I could make things bet-ter, but all I did was change where I would fail. Oh,

what do I do if I don't be-long where life can nev-er be a fair-y

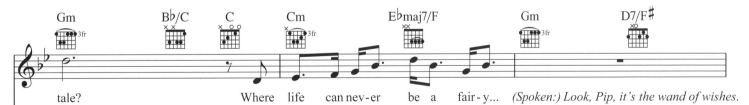

tale? Where life can nev-er be a fair-y... *(Spoken:) Look, Pip, it's the wand of wishes.*

FAIRYTALE LIFE
(After the Spell)

Music by ALAN MENKEN
Lyrics by STEPHEN SCHWARTZ

Dramatically

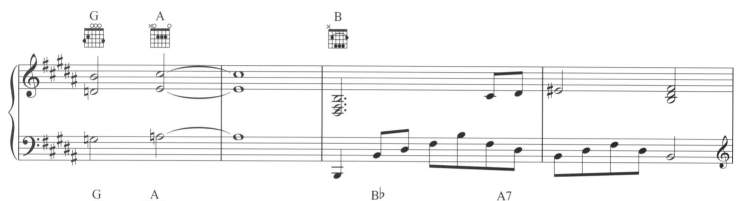

GISELLE:

Spoken: Well, it's not a very good morning at all, I'm afraid.

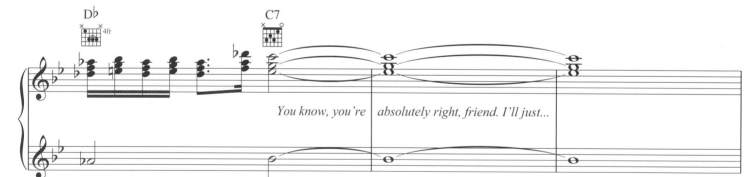

You know, you're absolutely right, friend. I'll just...

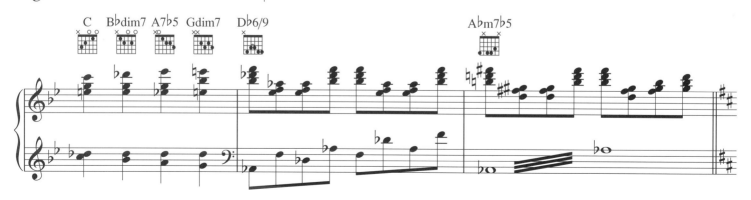

MORGAN:

Ah, _____ ah, _____ ah, _____ ah ha ha! This day is new now.

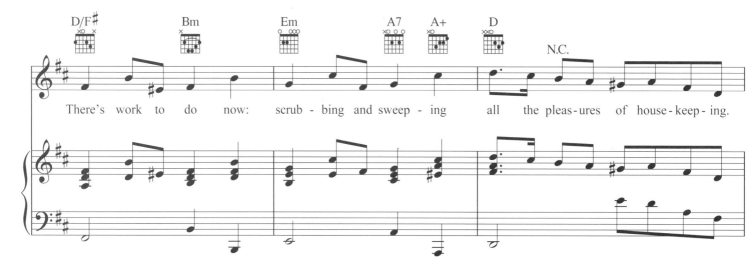

There's work to do now: scrub - bing and sweep - ing all the pleas - ures of house - keep - ing.

Cel - lar to at - tic, I'm just ec - stat - ic do - ing my dai - ly

chores. Let's sweep those floors!

Heroically

Spoken: *Giselle! You're even more beautiful than you were yesterday.*

ROBERT:
It's an-oth - er day, an -

oth - er quest. One more chance to

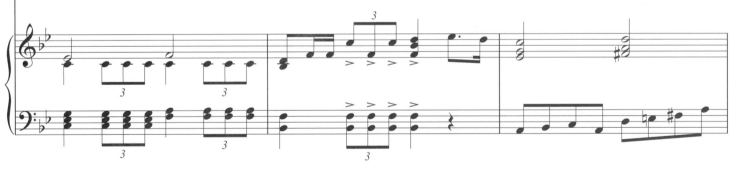

put my met - tle to the test!

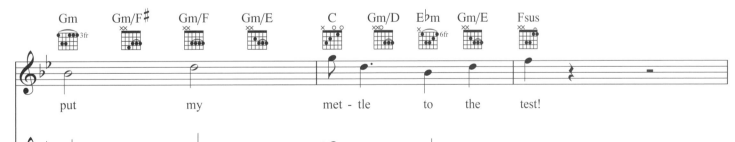

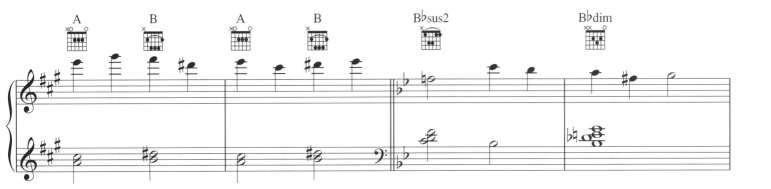

GISELLE:

Look all a-round us, life now will be

so full of song, love and laugh - ter. And you can bet we'll

fin - al - ly get our hap - pi - ly ev - er af -

ter.

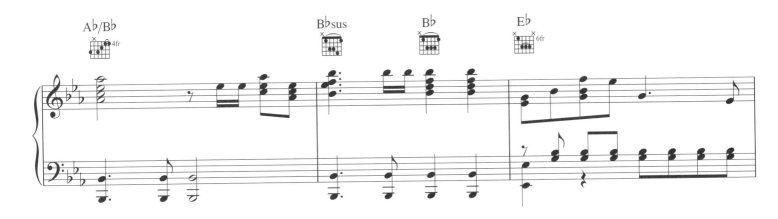

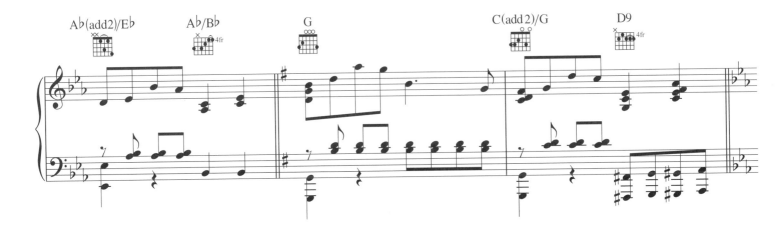

PERFECT

Music by ALAN MENKEN
Lyrics by STEPHEN SCHWARTZ

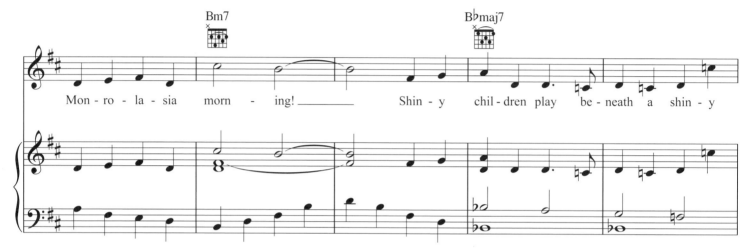

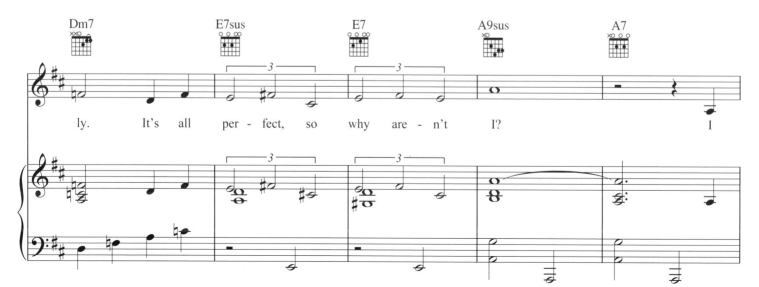

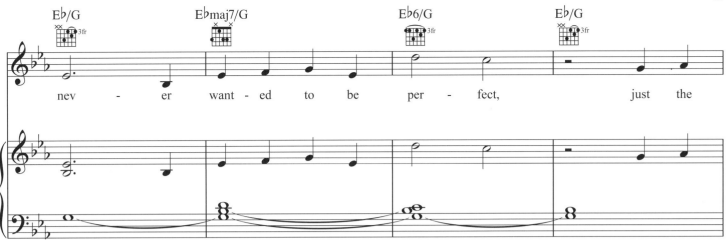

nev - er want - ed to be per - fect, just the

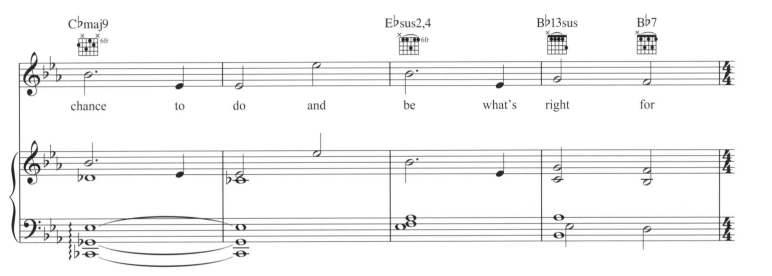

chance to do and be what's right for

me.

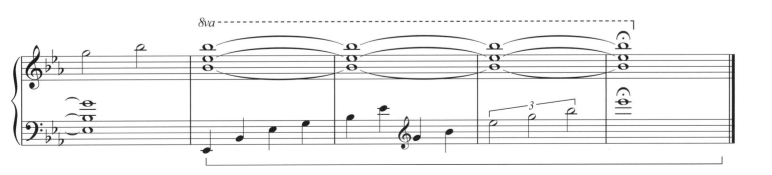

BADDER

Music by ALAN MENKEN
Lyrics by STEPHEN SCHWARTZ

MALVINA: Please don't fear that you are up-set-ting me.

GISELLE: Dear, I bare-ly know you're there. Sor-ry, were you speak-ing? You're hard to see... like a smell that lin-gers in the air.

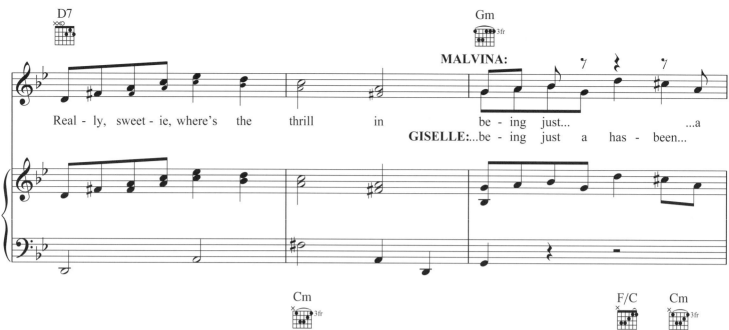

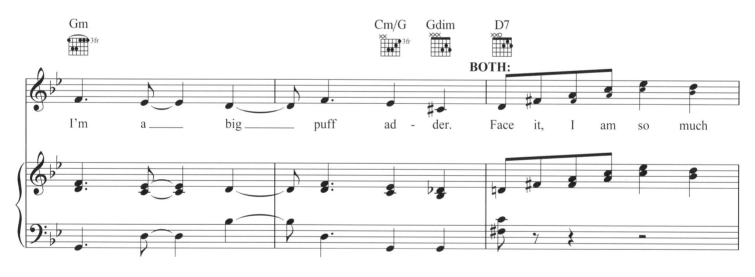

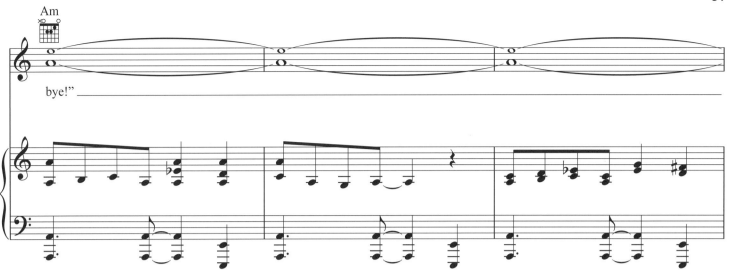

bye!" _____

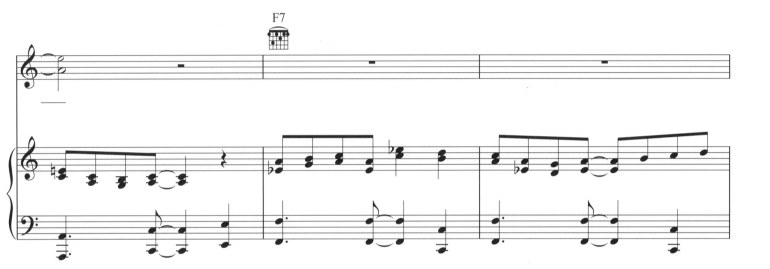

GISELLE:

Some-one real - ly should put a

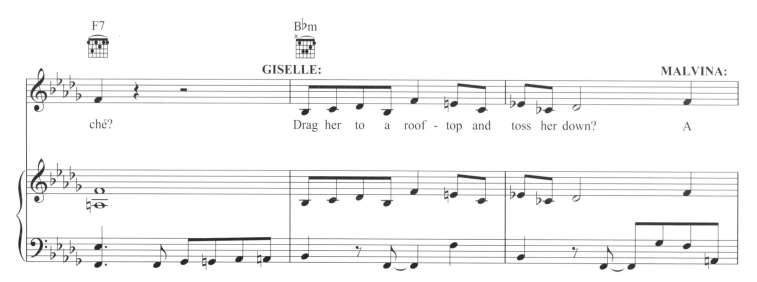

see that she lives hap-pi-ly NEV-ER af-ter! Once I ___ sit ___
___ a - lone a-top the ___ vil - lain lad - der,
ev-'ry-one in Mon-ro - la - sia will to-tal-ly be in my

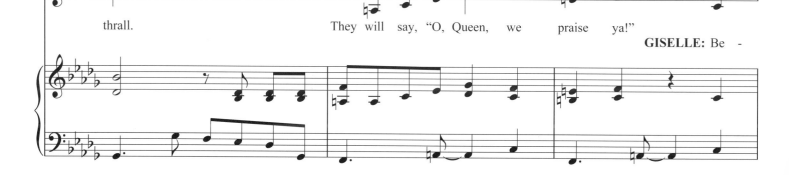

thrall. They will say, "O, Queen, we praise ya!"

GISELLE: Be -

LOVE POWER

Music by ALAN MENKEN
Lyrics by STEPHEN SCHWARTZ

Freely, with some urgency

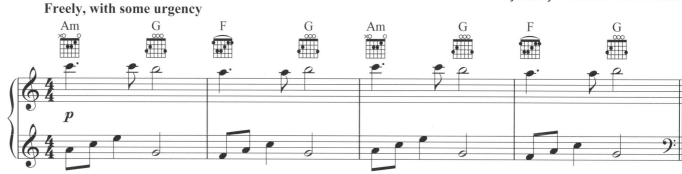

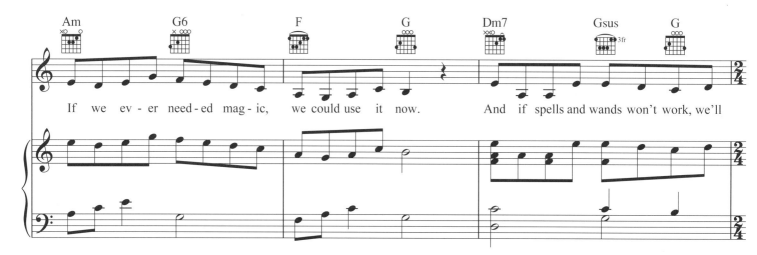

If we ev-er need-ed mag-ic, we could use it now. And if spells and wands won't work, we'll

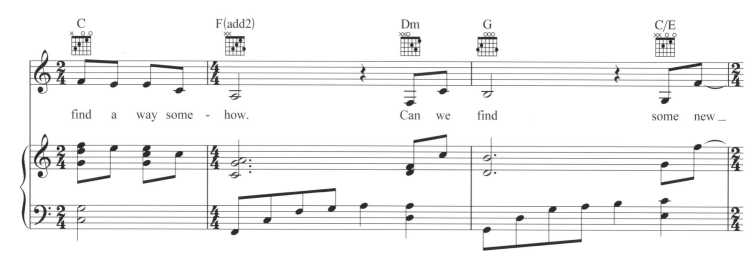

find a way some - how. Can we find some new _

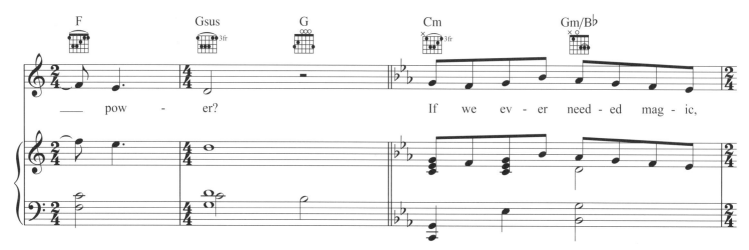

_ pow - er? If we ev - er need - ed mag - ic,

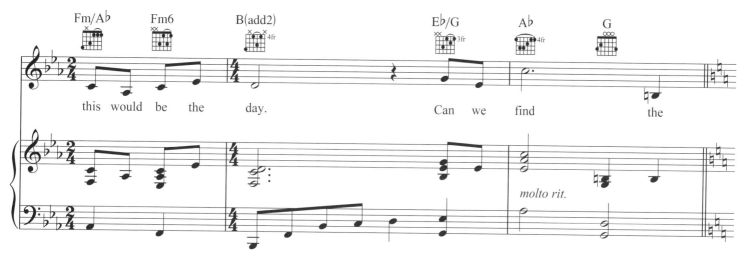

this would be the day. Can we find the

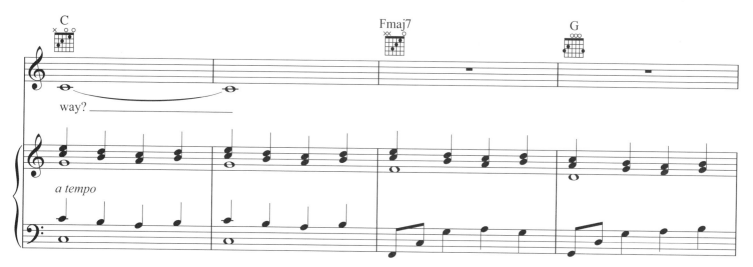

way? _____

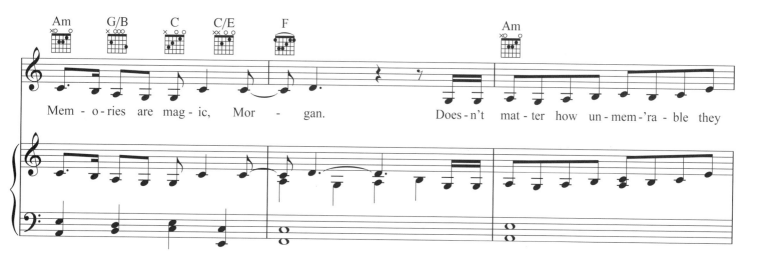

Mem - o - ries are mag - ic, Mor - gan. Does - n't mat - ter how un - mem - 'ra - ble they

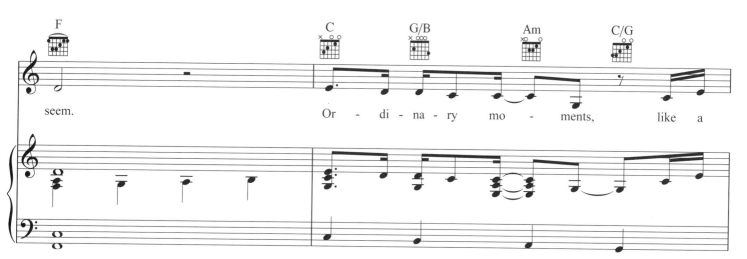

seem. Or - di - na - ry mo - ments, like a

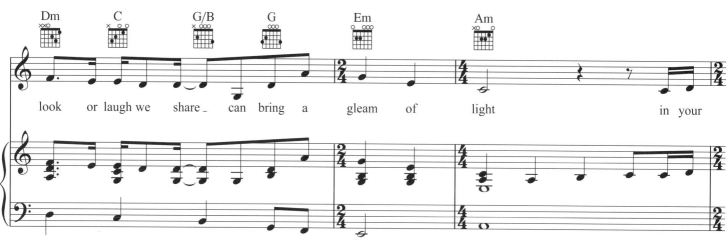

look or laugh we share _ can bring a gleam of light in your

bleak-est, dark-est ho-ur. _____ Mem-o-ries can save us, Mor-

-gan. When you add them up, ___ they paint a pic-ture

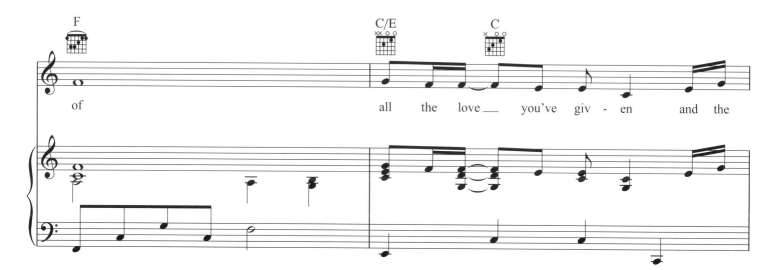

of all the love ___ you've giv-en and the

love you have _ re - ceived, and in that love, _____ there's pow -

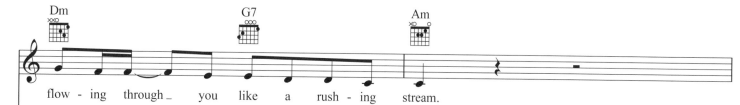

- er. _____ Love _____ pow - er. _____ Feel it

flow - ing through _ you like a rush - ing stream.

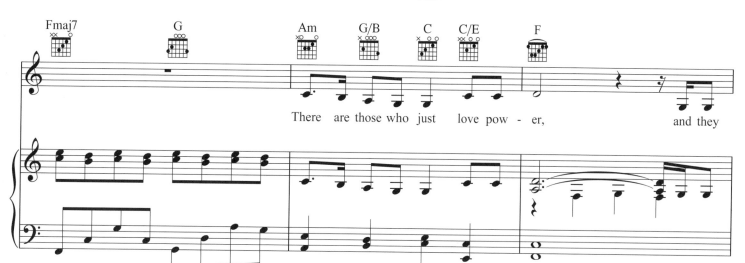

There are those who just love pow - er, and they

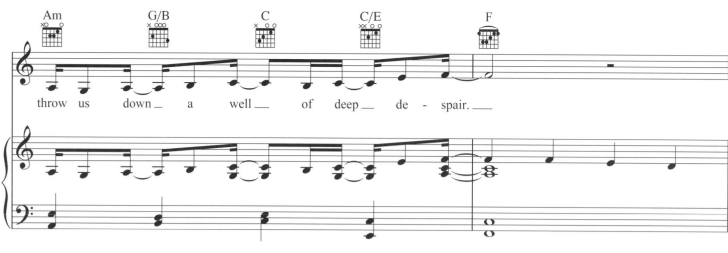

throw us down_ a well_ of deep_ de - spair._

They don't un-der-stand_ that while they live in hate and fear,_ look what's right

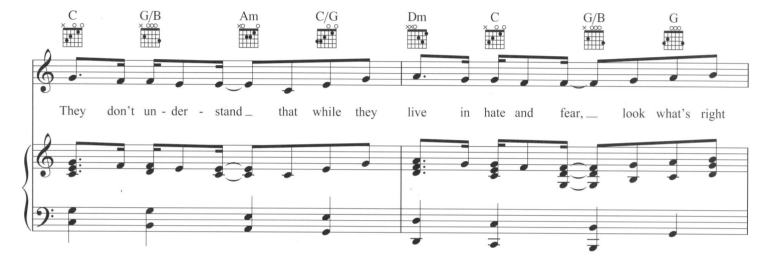

there: love pow - er._ Love,_____ love

pow- er. We can al-ways choose_ to use it if we___ dare.

mem-'ry seems to know. Let it grow, let it glow. Oh.

Oh. Oh.

Oh.

From a rock there grows a flow-

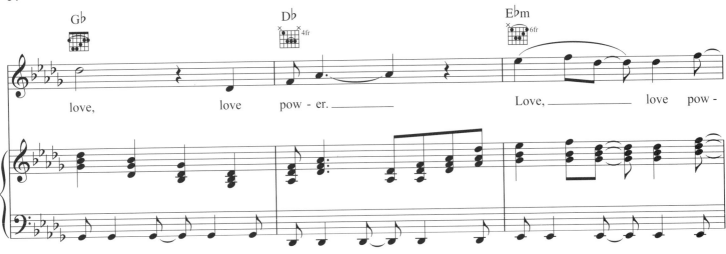

love, love pow - er. _____ Love, _____ love pow-

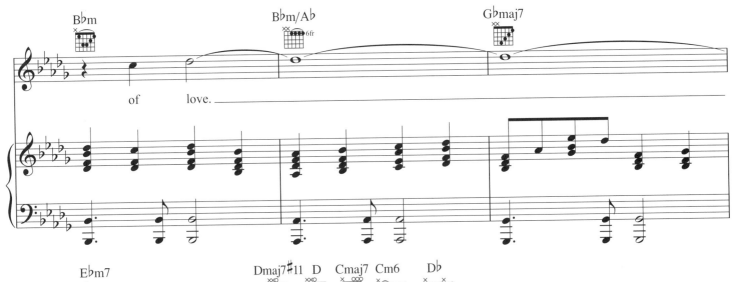

- er. _____ Just re - mem - ber _____ the mem - 'ries _____ that show us _____ the pow - er _____

of love. _____